D1073965

ROWAN BLANCHARD
TEEN ACTRESS

BY JEANNE MARIE FORD

Published by The Child's World®
1980 Lookout Drive • Mankato, MN 56003-1705
800-599-READ • www.childsworld.com

Photographs ©: Richard Shotwell/Invision/AP Images, cover, 1; Helga Esteb/
Shutterstock Images, 5, 8, 16; Sarah Edwards/WENN Ltd/Alamy, 6; AF archive/Alamy,
10; Quasar/starmaxinc.com/Newscom, 12; John Shearer/Invision/Mattel/AP Images,
14; Chris Pizzello/Invision/AP Images, 18; Matt Baron/BEI/Shutterstock Images, 20

ISBN 9781503819962
LCCN 2016960920

Printed in the United States of America
PA02335

ABOUT THE AUTHOR

Jeanne Marie Ford is an Emmy-winning TV scriptwriter who holds a master of
fine arts degree in writing for children from Vermont College. She has written
numerous children's books and articles. Ford also teaches college English.
She lives in Maryland with her husband and two children.

TABLE OF
CONTENTS

FAST FACTS

Name

- Rowan Eleanor Blanchard

Birthdate

- October 14, 2001

Birthplace

- Los Angeles, California

Fun Trivia

- Rowan is named after a character in a novel by Anne Rice.

- Rowan loves chocolate, show tunes, and baking. She is also a **pescatarian**.

- Some of Rowan's role models include Emma Watson, Audrey Hepburn, and Beyoncé.

- Rowan's favorite books include the Harry Potter series and *The Fault in Our Stars* by John Green. Her favorite band is the Beatles.

- Rowan says her perfect Los Angeles, California, day would include a walk outside in the rain and a trip to an art museum or a book store.

- Rowan's younger siblings, Carmen and Shane, are also actors.

Chapter 1

STARTING OUT

Rowan Blanchard lay still and tried to look dead. The hot studio lights beat down on her red velvet dress. Fighting the urge to blink or twitch, she blocked out the laughter from the studio audience. Playing Riley Matthews, who was playing Shakespeare's Juliet, was her biggest challenge yet as an actress.

Rowan had been acting almost her whole life. As a little girl, she dressed up as Cinderella. She twirled and danced to entertain her parents' friends. After her grandfather gave her a book about Broadway musicals, Rowan pored over it for hours at a time.

Rowan often hung out at her parents' yoga studio. It is a place where many Hollywood actors take classes.

◀ *Girl Meets World* **debuted on the Disney Channel on June 27, 2014.**

▲ Rowan began attending many red carpet events when
she started acting.

Her father, Mark, also directed and acted in plays. When she was five, Rowan begged him to let her become a professional actor. He said no. But she kept asking. Finally, he agreed to let her try.

Rowan clutched her teddy bear as she arrived at her first job acting in a television commercial. She remembers running through a forest, pretending to be terrified. But the commercial aired only in Russia. Rowan never even saw it.

For her next commercial, Rowan was supposed to ride a bike. But she had never learned to ride one. For two days, she wobbled around the set on two wheels. When filming started, she pedaled into the scene and hit her **mark** like an expert.

Over the next few years, Rowan filmed 20 commercials. But she was rejected by casting directors far more than she was hired. Often they said she was too young or too old or had the wrong hair color for a role. She used the disappointment as motivation. "All right, you'll just get the next one," she told herself.[1]

Chapter 2

BIG NEWS

Brightly colored squares covered the floor where Rowan squatted like a frog. She hopped up and down. "Can't stop going hippity-hop!"[2] she exclaimed to an imaginary robot. Then she opened her mouth wide and pretended to catch a fly.

Rowan thought acting in the series *Dance-A-Lot-Robot* was fun. But it wasn't exactly the big break she'd been hoping for. She later snagged a role in a television **pilot** called *Little in Common*. But the series never aired.

Then Rowan broke into films. She had a part in the movie *The Back-up Plan*. A beautiful woman strode up to her one day on the set. She was the movie's lead, superstar Jennifer Lopez. "Hi, Sweetie!"[3] she said.

◄ **Rowan was nominated for a Young Artist Award for her role in *Spy Kids: All the Time in the World*.**

▲ **Rowan at the premiere for *Spy Kids: All the Time in the World* in 2011.**

She drew Rowan into a hug. Rowan's part was small. She didn't even have any scenes with Lopez.

When she was eight, Rowan auditioned for a role in *Spy Kids: All the Time in the World*. Rowan was a huge fan of the first three films in the series. But she knew the odds of getting such a big role were slim.

When *Spy Kids* director Robert Rodriguez called her house, Rowan's mom, Elizabeth, was there.

She took a picture of the famous director's name on her caller identification screen. "There's someone special on the phone for you,"[4] she told her daughter. Rowan nervously took the phone. "Hello?" she asked, afraid it might be bad news. "Hi Rowan, it's Robert,"[5] he said before dropping the bombshell that she got the part.

Rodriguez adjusted the script to make Rowan's character, Rebecca, a prankster like Rowan. One day in the school trailer, Rowan and costar Mason Cook squeezed into a closet. Then they pretended they needed help. They shouted for someone to find them. They hid so well that no one found them for a long time.

Rowan did all of her own stunts in *Spy Kids*. With a harness, ropes, and a belly plate, she could fly. She soared from one piece of cushiony furniture to another. Special effects were later added to the huge **green screen** that glowed behind her.

When the movie **premiered**, it hardly felt real. She said, "I kept on thinking, 'That's not me up on the screen.'"[6]

Chapter 3

ROLE OF A LIFETIME

Rowan was disappointed. "I would cast you right now if it weren't for your age,"[7] producer Michael Jacobs told her. She had just read for the part of Maya in a new television comedy called *Girl Meets World*. Jacobs was looking for someone 15 or 16 years old. It was fall of 2012, and Rowan was only 11. She went out to her father's car and cried.

Two weeks later, Jacobs called her back. He had decided the main character should be younger. Rowan auditioned at least seven more times. Eventually, she switched parts with another actress, Sabrina Carpenter. Now Rowan was reading for the lead role, Riley Matthews. Sabrina was auditioning to play her best friend.

◀ **Rowan and Sabrina became friends after meeting at the audition for *Girl Meets World*.**

▲ Rowan with other members of the *Girl Meets World* cast in 2014. The show ended in early 2017.

"Go outside and bond,"[8] Jacobs finally told the two girls. They left the room and talked for 30 minutes about rock band Pink Floyd and actress Judy Garland. They became instant friends, just like the characters Riley and Maya in *Girl Meets World*.

Rowan was eating cake on her brother's birthday when she got the call that she had been **booked** for the part of Riley. She knew her whole life was about to change. *Girl Meets World* was a **spin-off** of a popular comedy from the 1990s called *Boy Meets World*.

Its stars were now grown up and playing Riley's parents. Rowan was born a year after the original show went off the air. Now she binge-watched every episode of the first series.

On Wednesdays, Rowan and her cast mates gathered around a table, eager to read each new episode's script. Rowan had butterflies in her stomach when the show started filming. But soon everyone settled into a rhythm.

After *Girl Meets World* first aired on June 27, 2014, Rowan was instantly famous. But Rowan said, "When I go home, I'm still a normal kid."[10] She shared a room with her sister and did chores. "Some kids play soccer," she said. "Some play football. I just love to act."[11]

"I want to play teens who are layered and intricate and complicated. I don't want to play roles that make us look dumb and annoying, because I know teens. I know we are intelligent and are here to change the world."[9]

—Rowan Blanchard

Chapter 4

LOOKING AHEAD

Rowan stood tall before a crowd of thousands. She was addressing a passionate crowd at WE Day in Minnesota in November of 2015. They were gathered to celebrate young people who were making a difference in the world. Behind her, photos flashed on a giant screen. "There's this big misconception that being a **feminist** only helps girls and women,"[12] she informed the audience. She was there to tell them otherwise.

Rowan appreciated the opportunity her fame gave her to make a difference. "You don't choose to become a role model," she noted. "It's just something that happens to you."[13]

◄ **Rowan has had many opportunities to speak to teens about how they can make a difference.**

Text inside image: Because you're worth it. L'ORÉAL PARIS — Benefiting Children — NITY FAIR

▲ Rowan continues to be an activist for many issues today.

When she was 13, Rowan wrote an essay on feminism that was widely read on social media. Like her own role model, Emma Watson, she spoke before the United Nations in January of 2016 about women's rights. Rowan has also been very vocal in her support for equal rights for all people, regardless of their gender or sexual orientation.

> "Acting's great, but school is the thing that stays with you forever."[14]
>
> —Rowan Blanchard

Magazine editors were so impressed by what she had to say that they began asking her to write for their publications.

Rowan dreams of attending an Ivy League college and then becoming a journalist someday. "I want to act, I want to write, I want to direct, I want to become a human rights lawyer, too," she said. "So I'll do them all at the same time!"[15]

THINK ABOUT IT

- Rowan Blanchard never took an acting class, though her father works as her acting coach. Do you think it is important for actors to study their craft?
- Rowan grew up in Los Angeles, which is where most films and television shows are made. If she lived somewhere else, how might her career have taken a different path?
- Rowan is passionate about many issues. If you had the ability to influence many people, what issues would you talk about?

Birds

Trudi Strain Trueit

Marshall Cavendish
Benchmark
New York

Other Marshall Cavendish Offices:

Marshall Cavendish International (Asia) Private Limited, 1 New Industrial Road, Singapore 536196 • Marshall Cavendish International (Thailand) Co Ltd. 253 Asoke, 12th Flr, Sukhumvit 21 Road, Klongtoey Nua, Wattana, Bangkok 10110, Thailand • Marshall Cavendish (Malaysia) Sdn Bhd, Times Subang, Lot 46, Subang Hi-Tech Industrial Park, Batu Tiga, 40000 Shah Alam, Selangor Darul Ehsan, Malaysia

Marshall Cavendish is a trademark of Times Publishing Limited

All websites were available and accurate when this book was sent to press.

Library of Congress Cataloging-in-Publication Data

Trueit, Trudi Strain.
Birds / Trudi Strain Trueit.
p. cm. — (Backyard safari)
Includes bibliographical references and index.
Summary: "Identify specific birds. Explore their behavior, life cycle, mating habits, geographical location, anatomy, enemies, and defenses"
—Provided by publisher.
ISBN 978-1-60870-242-8 (print) ISBN 978-1-60870-624-2 (ebook)
1. Birds—Juvenile literature. 2. Bird watching—Juvenile literature. I. Title.
QL676.2.T78 2012
598—dc22
2010044952

Editor: Christine Florie
Publisher: Michelle Bisson
Art Director: Anahid Hamparian
Series Designer: Alicia Mikles

Expert Reader: Gary Ritchison, Department of Biological Science, Eastern Kentucky University, Richmond, Kentucky

Photo research by Marybeth Kavanagh

Cover photo by *Tim Zurowski/All Canada Photos/photolibrary*
The photographs in this book are used by permission and through the courtesy of: *Alamy*: blickwinkel, 4; William Leaman, 8, 21TR; Andrew Darrington, 10; Arco Images GmbH, 11; Gary W. Carter, 20, 23TC; All Canada Photos, 21TC, 22TC; Rick & Nora Bowers, 22TR; Nigel Westwood, 26; Gay Bumgarner, 27; *SuperStock*: age fotostock, 5, 9, 14 (bottom), 17; NovaStock, 6; Bruce & Jan Lichtenberger, 7L; Barry Mansell, 7R; Larry Allen, 12; All Canada Photos, 21TL, 21LL, 21LC, 21LR, 22TL, 22LL, 23TL; IndexStock, 22LR; Tier und Naturfotografie, 23TR, 23LR; imagebroker.net, 23LL; *Photo Researchers, Inc.*: William H. Mullins, 15; *Media Bakery*: Corbis, 25; BigStockPhoto, 13R, 13L; *Cutcaster*: Ivan Montero, 14TC; Sergey Skryl, 14TL; Sergej Razvodovskij, 14TR

Printed in Malaysia (T)
1 3 5 6 4 2

Contents

Introduction

Have you ever watched baby spiders hatch from a silky egg sac? Or seen a butterfly sip nectar from a flower? If you have, you know how wonderful it is to discover nature for yourself. Each book in the Backyard Safari series takes you step-by-step on an easy outdoor adventure, then helps you identify the animals you've found. You'll also learn ways to attract, observe, and protect these valuable creatures. As you read, be on the lookout for the Safari Tips and Trek Talk facts sprinkled throughout the book. Ready? The fun starts just steps from your back door!

ONE

Wings of Wonder

Birds can be found nearly everywhere on Earth: circling mountain peaks, diving hundreds of feet beneath the sea, or hanging around your local fast-food restaurant. They are clever, energetic, resourceful, musical, and, of course, beautiful. Is it any wonder that watching birds is one of the world's most popular outdoor activities?

Life Begins

Birds are part of a larger group of animals called **vertebrates**, or animals with spinal columns. Other vertebrates include dogs, fish, and you!

Every bird's life begins in an egg. Usually, a female lays her egg(s) in a nest she has made from twigs, grasses, mud, or other natural materials. Hummingbirds also like to use spiderwebs in their nests. Ducks line their nests with their own feathers. Most backyard birds lay between four and ten eggs in a **clutch**.

This is an American robin's nest. Female robins make their nests out of mud mixed with grass or small twigs. A robin can lay up to six eggs per clutch.

Safari Tip
You find a baby bird on the ground. What do you do? If the **fledgling** is hopping around and calling, leave it alone. A parent is nearby. However, if the bird is very tiny, it may have fallen out of its nest. If you can easily and gently return it to the nest, it's okay to do that. It's not true that parents will reject a baby bird after it's been touched by a human. However, if the baby is injured or has been left alone for more than three hours, place it in a covered shoe box (with air holes) and take it to a wildlife rehabilitation center.

Depending on the type of bird, it may take anywhere from nine to forty days for the eggs to hatch.

Young birds will usually spend two to six weeks being raised by one or both parents. Once they learn to fly and find food, they are ready to strike out on their own. Survival, though, is a constant battle. Disease, starvation, and predators mean that only about two out of every ten birds will make it beyond a year. Most backyard songbirds live from three to six years.

Young robins are fed worms by their parents before they can fend for themselves.

Bundles of Energy

Whether flying or feeding, backyard birds are frequently on the go. To keep their energy levels up, birds must eat often. They have lightweight jaws called bills or beaks. Birds do not have teeth. The size and shape of a beak depends on a bird's diet. An owl's hooked beak is made for tearing apart meat. A hummingbird's long, narrow beak dips deep into flowers to drink **nectar**. A woodpecker's sturdy beak hammers into tree bark to reach the insects inside.

Trek Talk
Birds are the only animals on Earth with feathers.

Beaks come in a variety of shapes and sizes. For instance, an owl's beak is hooked (left) and a hummingbird's is long and slender (right).

Birds have excellent eyesight and hearing. They use their keen vision to find food. Their ears are located behind and slightly beneath each eye. Good hearing is important for communication and avoiding predators. Most birds make two types of sounds: long songs and short calls. A song is used for attracting a mate and defending territory. Calls can be used to identify family members, warn of predators, or share information about food.

A blue-winged warbler sings. It may be trying to attract a mate or to warn others of a predator.

Bird Brains

Magpies, crows, jays, and ravens belong to one of the smartest bird families. These birds learn quickly, have good memories, and often come up with creative plans to get food. On one street corner in Japan, crows hop into the crosswalk when the light turns red and drop walnuts they've picked from the nearby trees. They fly away when the light turns green and wait for the passing cars to crush the walnut shells. When the WALK signal flashes again and traffic stops, the crows head back out into the crosswalk to collect their meal!

Head

Crown

Eye

Tail

Beak

Wings

Breast

Legs

Toes

Claws

Birds share the same body features such as wings, tails, beaks, and claws.

Trek Talk

Did you know that birds can sleep while standing? When a bird lands on a perch, a tendon in each leg tightens and locks the toes in place. This keeps the bird from falling, even as it naps.

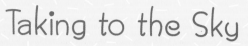

This photograph shows what a bird's wings look like in mid–flight.

Taking to the Sky

In the air, a bird can handle most any flying challenge, from a gentle glide to a steep dive. Birds are built for flight. Their bones are light yet strong. A bird's curved, hinged wings are formed by a series of small bones, much the way human arms are constructed. The bones are attached to powerful muscles in a bird's chest. A bird uses these chest muscles to flap its wings. With each downstroke, the wing pushes air downward, thrusting the bird forward and upward. On the upstroke, the hinged wings fold slightly inward. A hummingbird's wings sweep rapidly back and forth (about fifty beats per second!), allowing the bird to hover like a helicopter. Wings are covered by feathers, or **plumage**. Lightweight and waterproof, feathers aid in flight. They also act as insulation, keeping a bird cool in summer and warm in winter. Bird tails come in all sizes and shapes: square, round, forked, or pointed. Tails are used for stability, steering, and landing (they work like brakes).

Trek Talk

Small songbirds, such as wrens and sparrows, may fly up to 30 miles per hour, while larger birds, such as pigeons, fly at speeds of more than 60 miles per hour. The peregrine falcon (below) is the fastest animal on Earth. National Geographic once clocked one diving at 242 miles per hour!

Now that you know more about how birds live and fly it's time to put your knowledge to good use. Let's safari!

TWO

You Are the Explorer

The great thing about bird-watching, or **birding**, is that you can do it any time of year. Each season offers something special to see. In spring many birds are **migrating**, or heading north from their warm, winter feeding grounds. Watch for a variety of birds passing through your area. Summer is the time to search for birds nesting and fledglings learning to feed and fly. During the autumn months, migrating birds begin the journey south, again giving you more great viewing opportunities. Also watch for changes in plumage color in the fall. Many birds will **molt**, or lose their bright summer feathers. Their new feathers tend to match the muted browns and golds of the season. In winter a white backdrop of snow makes it easier to spot smaller birds that may not migrate, such as chickadees, goldfinches, and sparrows.

Trek Talk
Measuring up to 4 inches from beak to tail, hummingbirds are the smallest birds in the world.

Pick a day for your safari when it isn't raining or snowing. The best time to go is before 11 AM. The morning is when most birds are out hunting for food. This is also when they are most vocal, making it easier for you to see and hear them. Take a friend or sibling along. Two sets of eyes and ears are better than one!

Make Your Safari Count

Why not safari for science? For four days each February bird lovers from across North America head outdoors to spot as many birds as they can. The event is called the Great Backyard Bird Count. Participants enter their figures online, and scientists tally and post the results. Experts use the information to track changes in bird populations, migration patterns, and diseases, and to aid in conservation efforts. To find out how to be a part of the Great Backyard Bird Count visit www.birdsource.org/gbbc.

What Do I Wear?

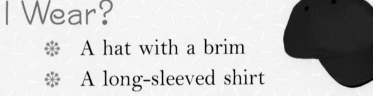

* A hat with a brim
* A long-sleeved shirt
* Jeans or long pants
* A sweater or coat (if the weather is cold)
* Hat, gloves, and boots (in winter)
* Sunglasses
* Sunscreen

What Do I Take?

* Binoculars
* Digital camera
* Notebook
* Colored pens or pencils
* Blanket or towel to sit on (in winter)
* Water

Where Do I Go?

Find a spot in your backyard that is attractive to birds. They will be looking for:

* Flowers—to feed on nectar, seeds, and insects
* Grass—to eat seeds, insects, and worms
* Trees—to eat fruit, rest, and nest
* Bushes—to eat berries, rest, and nest
* Tree stumps and logs—to eat insects, rest, and nest
* Water, such as a stream, mud puddle, or birdbath

Backyard gardens with flowers, grass, and bushes attract many birds.

If your backyard doesn't offer these features, here are some other good safari locations:

* ❋ Meadows
* ❋ Open woodlands
* ❋ Fields and wetlands
* ❋ Public parks
* ❋ Lakes
* ❋ Garden nurseries

Always have an adult with you if you are going beyond your backyard.

What Do I Do?

❋ Find a spot where you'll get a good, clear view of the area and sit down. Slowly scan the area with your binoculars. Look at all levels: on the ground, in the flowers and bushes, and in the trees. Keep as still and quiet as you can.

Be sure to watch for birds in clear viewing areas. Don't forget to bring a pair of binoculars.

❋ Take a photo or make a sketch of any birds you see. You will probably know some birds, such as the cardinal or American robin, right away. For these, simply write down the name of the bird and keep count of how many you see.

Make a full entry for the birds you don't know. Ask yourself: What are the bird's main colors? What are its **field marks** (spots, stripes, color patches) and where are they located (head, chest, wings, tail)? Is the bird small (about the size of a sparrow), medium (robin), or large (crow)? What is the color and shape of its beak? Describe its tail, too. Is the bird singing or doing anything? Leave a blank line at the bottom of your entry to add its name later.

BIRD

Color(s): black back with white patch down the center, white chest, black-and-white striped head

Wings: black with white spots

Field marks: swish of red on the back of the head

Size: medium (robin sized)

Beak: long, straight

Song: *peek, peek, peek*

Activity: perched on side of tree trunk, drilling bark for insects

Count: 1

Name: _____

Your Drawing or Photo Goes Here

Safari Tip

A bird can be here and gone in a flash. But a quick glimpse of its head may be all you need to identify it. Note the head's main color(s) and any field marks, such as stripes, spots, or eye rings. Are the field marks over the eye? Around it? Does the crown have a **crest** (see above)? How about the beak? What is its color and shape?

❊ Listen! Many birds will be hidden in the trees or bushes. You may only be able to hear the *cheep-cheep* of a sparrow, the *what cheer* of a cardinal, or the rapid *rat-a-tat-a-tat* of a woodpecker chipping away at bark. Crows and jays will often send out a loud *caw-caw-caw* or *jay-jay-jay* to warn when eagles, hawks, or other predators are near. Write down what you hear in your notebook. With practice you'll be able to tell which birds are close by their songs and calls.

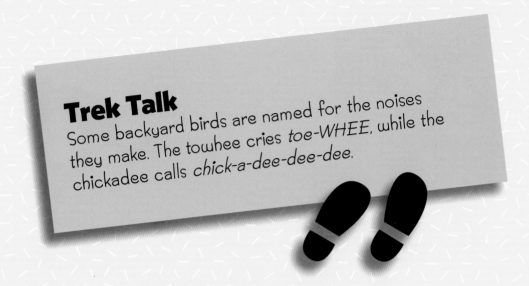

Trek Talk
Some backyard birds are named for the noises they make. The towhee cries *toe-WHEE*, while the chickadee calls *chick-a-dee-dee-dee*.

❋ Spend about a half hour to an hour on safari.
❋ Clean up the area, and take all your belongings with you when you leave.

Did you have fun? Don't worry if you didn't see many birds. The more you safari, the better you'll become at hearing and seeing these swift animals. At home, download your photos onto the computer and print them. It's time to learn more about your backyard visitors.

THREE
A Guide to Birds

Now that your safari is over, let's work to identify the birds you saw. Select an entry from your notebook. If you took a photo, paste it next to its description. Compare your photo and entry to the birds in the guide that follows. Search in this order:

* Main colors
* Field marks: spots, stripes, speckles, or other noticeable features
* Size: small (sparrow), medium (robin), or large (crow)
* Tail shape and color
* Beak shape and color

BIRD

Color(s): black back with white patch down the center, white chest, black-and-white striped head

Wings: black with white spots

Field marks: swish of red on the back of the head

Size: medium (robin sized)

Beak: long, straight

Song: *peek, peek, peek*

Activity: perched on side of tree trunk, drilling bark for insects

Count: 1

Name: hairy woodpecker

Did you find a match? If so, fill in the blank at the bottom of your entry. If not, don't get discouraged. North America is home to more than eight hundred different kinds of birds—far too many to show here! Use the resources at the back of this book for more help in identifying your birds.

Bird Guide

Northern Cardinal

House Finch

Ruby-Throated Hummingbird

Blue Jay

Steller's Jay

American Robin

Bird Guide

Cedar Waxwing

House Sparrow

Song Sparrow

House Wren

Black-Capped Chickadee

Bird Guide

Dark-Eyed Junco

Hairy Woodpecker

European Starling

Red-Winged Blackbird

American Crow

FOUR

Try This!
Projects You Can Do

Birds are not only beautiful to watch, they are valuable, too. Birds help distribute seeds so that new plants may grow. They also pollinate trees and plants. They can help keep insect, worm, and spider populations under control. Birds also tell us a great deal about the health of our environment. When groups of birds get sick or die, this can signal that there are problems with the quality of our air, water, and soil. Here are some fun projects you can do to help keep Earth's birds singing well into the future.

Trek Talk—Troubled Times

The National Audubon Society says that several common North American birds are in trouble. In just the last forty years, some types of birds have lost as much as 80 percent of their population! Eastern and western meadowlarks, rufous hummingbirds, evening grosbeaks, and whip-poor-wills are among those that are most at risk. What's going on? Scientists say that land development, pollution, logging, and **global warming** are taking a deadly toll on our birds.

Pinecone Feeders

Help birds survive the winter with these easy-to-make pinecone feeders. You'll need a few large pinecones, a ball of twine, a bag of birdseed, and a jar of peanut butter (peanut butter is a good source of protein for birds). First, cut a piece of twine about 1 foot in length. Knot the middle of the twine around the stem of the pinecone near the top. Next, tie the ends of the twine together to form a loop. This will be your hanger. Pour some birdseed into a large mixing bowl. Holding the pinecone by its stem, use a butter knife to spread a thick layer of peanut butter onto the entire pinecone (be sure to get it into all of the nooks and crannies). Next, roll the pinecone in the bowl of birdseed until the peanut butter is completely

To make a pinecone feeder, choose a large pinecone that you can cover easily with peanut butter and birdseed.

coated. That's it! Your pinecone feeder is ready to hang on a tree branch or shrub in your backyard. Try placing different-sized pinecone feeders at different heights. You're likely to get plenty of hungry (and grateful) winged friends stopping by all winter long.

Spring Nesting Kit

A single bird will make more than a hundred trips to collect the grass, twigs, and other materials it needs for its nest. You can help by making a kit that offers birds some of their favorite nesting supplies. Collect some or all of these items:

You can help birds build their nests by hanging a nesting kit from a tree in your backyard full of items they can use to construct their nest.

❉ Tiny pieces of yarn, twine, or cotton string (3 inches or less; longer lengths may entangle birds)

❉ Small bits of cotton (break apart a cotton ball)

❉ Dog or cat fur

❉ Human hair

❉ Thin twigs (3 inches or less in length)

❉ Pine needles

Do not use anything made of plastic or nylon that isn't **biodegradable**, such as fishing line. Place the materials in an empty **suet feeder**. In early March, hang the nesting kit from a tree. Refill the kit as needed. Some birds will make more than one nest during the summer. It's fun to see which nesting materials certain birds prefer!

26

Summer Bird Garden

Did you know that hummingbirds love red flowers? It's easy to plant a pretty garden that will feed the birds, too. Choose six to eight plants from the Bird Favorites Plant List on the next page. These plants appeal to the most common birds in North America (they will also attract the spiders and insects that other birds eat).

Pick a sunny spot for your garden that has trees nearby. Use good soil. Add a birdbath by filling an old metal pie plate with about 1 inch of water. Weigh it down with a large rock on which birds can perch while they drink and bathe. Water your garden and fill the birdbath every few days. Don't use pesticides. Keep dogs and cats indoors or on a leash. Also, after the flowers bloom, don't cut off the heads. They will provide birds with seeds through the fall and winter. Cut back the plants in the spring. Enjoy your blooms and birds!

Place a birdbath in your yard. They're a great way to attract many birds.

Bird Favorites Plant List

BIRD	PLANTS
Cardinal	Impatiens, Zinnia, Sunflower
Chickadee	Black-eyed Susan, Sunflower, Zinnia
Cedar waxwing	Blueberry, Cotoneaster
Finch	Cosmos, Sunflower, Zinnia
Hummingbird	Red sage, Crocosmia, Trumpet vine
Junco	Marigold, Purple coneflower, Violet
American robin	Blueberry, Cotoneaster
Sparrow	Black-eyed Susan, Marigold, Sunflower

Once you start bird-watching, you may never want to stop. That's okay! Many people like it so much, they begin keeping track of every different bird they see. This is called a life list. Imagine how many types of birds a person could see in a whole lifetime! Why not find out? Thanks to your safari notebook, you are well on your way. Happy birding!

Glossary

biodegradable   material that will naturally break down, or decompose

birding   watching birds in their natural habitats

clutch   the number of eggs produced by a female bird at one time

crest   a tuft of feathers on top of a bird's head

field marks   spots, bars, stripes, or other distinguishing plumage marks on a bird

fledgling   a young bird that has just left the nest

global warming   an increase in Earth's average temperature that causes changes in climate that may result from human pollution

migrating   moving from one region to another

molt   when birds shed feathers that will be replaced by new growth

nectar   the sweet liquid secreted by plants

plumage   feathers

suet feeder   a metal cage-like bird feeder containing a block of lard filled with seeds, nuts, berries, and other food for wild birds

vertebrates   animals with spinal columns

Find Out More

Books

Allison, Sandy, ed. *Backyard Birds and Bird Feeding: 100 Things to Know.*
  Mechanicsburg, PA: Stackpole Books, 2007.
Solway, Andrew. *Eagles and Other Birds.* Chicago, IL: Heinemann Library, 2007.
Vanner, Michael. *A Field Guide to the Birds of North America.* Bath, UK: Parragon, 2007.

DVD

Adventures in Birdwatching, Animal Planet, 2007.

Websites

Cornell Lab of Ornithology: All About Birds

www.allaboutbirds.org

Use the bird guide to identify birds by sight and sound. Explore the photo gallery, listen to bird calls, and learn to improve your bird photography. You can even upload your own bird images to share.

The Great Backyard Bird Count

www.birdsource.org/gbbc

Discover how you can get involved in this annual count of North American birds. Print a handy checklist of the most common birds in your specific area to use for the count or any time!

National Audubon Society

www.audubon.org

Log on for detailed descriptions of nearly every bird in North America. See the list of birds that are slowly disappearing from our landscape and learn what you can do to make a difference.

Index

Page numbers in **boldface** are illustrations.

Meet the Author

TRUDI STRAIN TRUEIT welcomes various birds, including hummingbirds, juncos, chickadees, pine siskins, and jays, to her yard with feeders, birdbaths, and nesting kits. Her three cats like birding, too, but have to be content with doing all their viewing from inside! An award-winning journalist, Trudi has written more than sixty fiction and nonfiction books for children. She is the author of four other books in the Backyard Safari series, including *Spiders, Caterpillars and Butterflies,* and *Squirrels.* Trudi lives in Everett, Washington, with her husband, Bill, a high school photography teacher (and bird lover). Visit her website at www.truditrueit.com.